THE REICHSTAG FIRE, 1933

The spectacular fire in the German parliament, known as the Reichstag, on the night of February 27, 1933, put Adolf Hitler's drive for supreme power into high gear. The arson may have been the work of a distorted mind, an unfortunate malcontent. It may have been the signal for a Communist uprising, as the Nazis charged. Or was it a provocation not too cleverly arranged by the Fuehrer's own henchmen? The evidence that has accumulated over the years still leaves an element of doubt as to who was guilty and who was innocent in the Reichstag conflagration. What cannot be doubted, however, is that Hitler utilized the arson to justify his brutal suppression of every democratic right in Germany in his goose-step march to dictatorship.

PRINCIPALS

GEORGI DIMITROV – Bulgarian, international Communist, head of the Bulgarian Communist party from 1944 to 1949

PAUL JOSEPH GOEBBELS – Nazi propaganda chief

HERMANN GOERING – Leading Nazi, Minister of the Interior, head of the German Air Force (Luftwaffe), which he recreated and regenerated

PAUL ·VON HINDENBURG – Chief of German General Staff from 1916 to 1918, architect of major German victories in World War I, President of the German Republic

ADOLF HITLER – Fuehrer, chancellor, and eventual dictator of Germany

MARINUS VAN DER LUBBE – Dutch ex-Communist, accused of setting the fire

ERNST TORGLER – Leader of the Communist deputies in the Reichstag (German parliament)

THE REICHSTAG FIRE

February, 1933
Hitler Utilizes Arson
to Extend His Dictatorship

By Henry Gilfond

A World Focus Book

FRANKLIN WATTS, INC.
NEW YORK | 1973

Frontispiece: Berlin, the night of February 27, 1933. Flames sweep up to destroy the central cupola of the Reichstag as gutted Sessions Chambers blaze below.

COVER DESIGN BY NICK KRENITSKY

PHOTOGRAPHS COURTESY OF:
Charles Phelps Cushing: pp. 8, 27, 52; Library of Congress: pp. 20, 28, 34, 40, 43, 48; National Archives: pp. ii, viii, 13, 60, 63, 68, 70, 73 (top and bottom), 74

LIBRARY OF CONGRESS CATALOGING
IN PUBLICATION DATA

Gilfond, Henry.
    The Reichstag fire, February, 1933.

    (A World focus book)
    SUMMARY: Presents the background, events, and aftermath of the night the German parliament building burned.
    1. Berlin. Reichstagsgebäude–Fire, 1933–Juvenile literature. 2. National socialism–Juvenile literature. 3. Hitler, Adolf, 1889-1945–Juvenile literature. [1. Germany–History–20th century. 2. Hitler, Adolf, 1889-1945] I. Title.
DD256.5.G47   943.086   72-8182
ISBN 0-531-02168-8

Contents

For Jennifer, Christopher,
and Santiago Enrique

The Reichstag Fire

The German parliament building, or Reichstag, as it appeared some years before the fire. Before the entrance, atop a pedestal, the statue of the great German statesman Otto von Bismarck gazes northward. To the right and rear of the building, out of the photograph, are the Brandenburg Gate and the famous Unter den Linden.

An Ugly Building in Berlin

Ernst Torgler, the leader of the Communist party representatives in the Reichstag, was the last elected official to leave the imposing building on the night of February 27, 1933. It was the night of the sensational fire that marked the acceleration of Hitler's drive for supreme power. The Reichstag was the name of the German parliament in Berlin. It was also the name given to the ungainly structure where this lawmaking body met.

Paul Wallot, its architect, had labored for ten years, from 1884 to 1894, and had spent 87 million gold marks in its construction. He produced a sprawling building, erected on huge sandstone blocks, 460 feet long and 330 feet wide. Each corner of the structure had its own 130-foot tower. At its center was a massive glass cupola topped by a golden crown, some 250 feet from the ground.

The Berliners — known for their colorful nicknames — called this glass cupola the "biggest round cheese in Europe." They may have admired the rich wood panels of the interior and the expensive tapestries hung on the walls, but the Reichstag was also called "a house without any weather." This was because the sun never penetrated its windows efficiently and its rooms were always dimly lit and gloomy. The building consisted of a number of private offices for the legislators and larger meeting rooms, a restaurant, a reading room, and an oversized Sessions Chamber where 600 to 700 deputies introduced legislation, debated it, and either passed or defeated it.

From the day the building on Königsplatz (later Platz der Republik) in Berlin was completed, the people of Germany called for its demolition, its destruction. It was an ugly, pompous structure. At best, it was a poor imitation of the magnificent Belgian Palace of Justice in Brussels. Its destruction came on the night of February 27, 1933, but not as too many Germans may have expected.

Prelude to Burning

At ten minutes past eight o'clock in the evening Rudolf Scholz, a night watchman at the Reichstag, began his nightly rounds of the building. He walked from floor to floor, closing any windows left open, turning off any lights left on, closing the doors, and checking to see that there were no prowlers in any of the rooms. There was an underground passageway leading out of the Reichstag, with three doors by which the building might be entered or left. One door led to the boiler house, the house that provided the heating for the Reichstag. Another door led to the Reichstag cellar. The third door opened into the private apartment of the president of the Reichstag. In 1933, the president of the Reichstag was Hermann Goering, Hitler's right-hand man and Minister of the Interior.

Scholz did his job methodically. At about half-past eight, he came to the Sessions Chamber. He looked into the huge room, saw that everything was in order, began to proceed down the hall, then suddenly stopped. He had heard the sound of footsteps in the dark.

Quickly, apprehensively, he turned on the lights. There was a woman in the hall, Anna Rehme, the secretary to the Communist deputies. She told Scholz that she was going to the Communist office to pick up some election material. He watched her disappear around a bend in the hall, turned off the lights, and continued on his rounds.

Scholz finished his tour at 8:38, just as Ernst Torgler, with Wilhelm Koenen, another Communist deputy, and Anna Rehme were about to leave the building. Torgler said a few pleasant words to Scholz — they had known each other for a long time — then gave the night watchman his keys, and left.

Scholz was alone in the Reichstag, except for Albert Wendt, the night porter.

At quarter to nine, the Reichstag postman, Willi Otto, arrived at the parliament building to pick up the outgoing mail. He was met by the night porter who lit his lantern and led him up the main staircase to the Reichstag post office. About ten minutes later, at 8:55, his job done, Otto turned up his collar about his neck and walked out into a sharp wind and a temperature of 22°. The Reichstag was, for all purposes, dark and deserted. It was not, however, to remain dark and deserted for very long.

Fire!

Hans Floter, a theology student, had spent part of that evening at the State Library, near the Reichstag. He was on his way home. At about three minutes past nine, no more than thirteen minutes after the postman Willi Otto had left the Reichstag, Floter turned at the corner of the building and began to cross the square in front of its main entrance. Suddenly, there was a shattering of glass. Floter turned quickly, looked back and up at the Reichstag where the crash had come from. What the student saw must have chilled his blood. There was a man on the first-floor balcony, outside a window and to the right of the main entrance. In the man's hand was a burning torch.

Floter recovered from his shock quickly. He rushed off to find a police officer. He found Sergeant Karl Buwert who could not quite believe what the divinity student was trying to tell him. When the sergeant finally arrived in front of the Reichstag, the man was no longer on the balcony. But the window was indeed broken and there was an ominous red glow flickering behind it.

The divinity student, apparently satisfied that he had done his duty, had departed. But two other civilians, attracted by the noise of the shattering glass, now stood in front of the building with the police sergeant. Momentarily paralyzed with amazement, they watched the man now inside the Reichstag rush from window to window with the fiery torch in his hand.

"Why don't you shoot?" shouted one of the bystanders to the sergeant.

Buwert drew his gun, aimed, and fired.

The man in the Reichstag disappeared from the windows.

Buwert turned to another bystander, told him to go to the

5

nearest police station for help. "Tell them to call the fire brigade. The Reichstag is on fire."

Then Buwert himself ran off to get whatever help he could find. He met a soldier. He sent him off, too, to a police station to report the fire.

Meanwhile, he was joined by other passersby who were all shouting, "Police! Fire!"

They ran into Otto Schaeske, caretaker of the German Engineering Institute, coming out of that building.

"The Reichstag is on fire! Call the fire brigade!" they cried.

And all the while, the man with the torch was lighting up more rooms of the Reichstag in flames.

Other policemen, attracted by Sergeant Buwert's shot and by the general clamor, arrived on the scene, but it was not until Police Lieutenant Emil Lateit appeared that any really organized action began.

Lateit asked Buwert whether the fire brigade had been called. He ordered Buwert to sound the full-scale alarm. At the same time, he ordered the police sergeant to keep a close eye on the Reichstag windows and to fire at any suspicious movement within.

Next the lieutenant tried to open a door into the Reichstag, but could not manage it. Albert Wendt, the night porter, told him that Alexander Scranowitz, the house inspector, was on his way with the keys. Scranowitz had been at dinner in some friends' house nearby. Wendt had tried to reach him on the phone, but had not been able to. It was Scranowitz who had finally called Wendt. He had heard the fire engines.

"The restaurant is on fire!" Wendt shouted into the mouthpiece.

"Why didn't you call me?" Scranowitz shouted back.

He slammed down the receiver on its hook and rushed to the scene of the fire.

Opening the inner doors of the building, he ran up the stairs. Lateit and two of his men followed.

As they rushed into the lobby, they saw a red glow coming from beyond the Reichstag monument to Kaiser Wilhelm. Through the glass windows, they could see the flames in the huge Sessions Chamber. The curtains were burning. So were the wood panels and the carpets. The Reichstag restaurant was now a mass of flames.

Lieutenant Lateit ordered his men to draw their guns. A third constable named Poeschel had joined him. The lieutenant ordered his men to make a thorough search of the building. By now he was certain that the fire was the work of an arsonist.

The three policemen, their guns drawn, began to search for the culprit. Patrolman Poeschel was with House Inspector Scranowitz when the latter shut the door to the Sessions Chamber. They ran across the corridor to the large hall named in honor of the great Prussian statesman Otto von Bismarck. Suddenly, from the rear of the Sessions Chamber, a man cut across their path. And, just as suddenly, he stopped and then started to run back. Evidently he had seen Poeschel and Scranowitz and had wanted to escape from them.

But Poeschel aimed his gun at the man, who was bare to the waist, and shouted: "Hands up!"

The man raised his hands. But he made no other move and put up no resistance.

Poeschel frisked him and found a pocket knife, a wallet, and a passport.

"Why did you do it?" yelled Scranowitz at the arsonist, and struck him with his fists.

"As a protest," muttered the captive.

Berlin police inspect the charred ruins of the Reichstag restaurant.

According to his papers, the man was Marinus van der Lubbe. He was twenty-four years old and came from Leydon, Holland.

Patrolman Poeschel marched him out of the building at exactly twenty-seven minutes past nine, just twenty-four minutes after the fire had been discovered by the theology student.

Goering, Goebbels, and Hitler at the Scene

At the time of the fire, Paul von Hindenburg was dining with Franz von Papen, Vice-Chancellor of the Reich. Von Hindenburg had been Chief of the German Staff in World War I after August 1916 and was now President of the German Republic. The two men were eating at the Herrenklub, one of the more exclusive dining clubs in Berlin, and it was just around the corner from the Reichstag.

That evening Hermann Goering, who had been the last commander of the famous Richthofen Flying Squadron in World War I and was now President of the Reichstag and Hitler's Minister of the Interior, was occupied in his private office.

Adolf Hitler was at the home of his Minister of Propaganda, Paul Joseph Goebbels. Less than a month before, Hitler had become Chancellor of the Reich, most powerful parliamentary position in Germany. The club-footed Goebbels was entertaining his Fuehrer with an evening of Hitler's favorite music.

Count Wolf von Helldorf was leader of the Berlin-Brandenburg Storm Troopers, Hitler's private army, and was responsible for Hitler's safety. He was out on the town with an aide, making the rounds of his favorite bars and wine cellars.

All the top men in both the government and the Nazi party, except for Heinrich Himmler, deputy leader of the Schutzstaffel (Hitler's Defense Corps) and director of Hitler's Gestapo (Secret Police), were in the vicinity of the Reichstag or near enough to get there in a hurry when the building started to blaze. They were all to be at the scene within minutes.

Von Papen, at the Herrenklub, heard a sudden shouting

in the streets. Looking out of the window from his table he saw a strange red glow in the sky. One of the waiters hurried up to him and whispered, "The Reichstag is on fire!"

Von Papen hurried to the window to get a better look. Red flames and swirls of smoke were shooting out of the glass dome of the building.

"The Reichstag is on fire," von Papen repeated to the old general. If von Hindenburg was alarmed by the news, or in any way upset, he did not show it to von Papen.

The Vice-Chancellor put the old man into his own car and told his chauffeur to drive the President home. He then hurried over to the burning building.

Goering was already there. A captain of the Berlin police had brought the news of the fire to him, and the flamboyant minister had rushed to his car. The police had cordoned off the area in the vicinity of the Reichstag and Goering's car was stopped, but not for long. No one in Berlin stopped the Minister of the Interior.

Goering found one of the doors to the building locked. He tried another, found it open, and walked in. A number of news-papermen had discovered this open door as well, but Goering ordered them all out.

The head of the fire-fighting team hurried over to make a report on the progress they were making. Goering brushed him off and told him to keep on fighting the blaze. He further ordered someone to inform Hitler and the chief of police of what was happening; then he headed for his own rooms in the Reichstag.

On his way there, von Papen joined him.

"This is a Communist crime!" Goering shouted to him.

Von Papen was a Catholic, a conservative, and an aristo-crat who intensely disliked associating with the Nazis, or anyone of their kind. He had tried desperately to keep Hitler out of the

11

Chancellorship, preferring an aristocratic rule in Germany. The one thing he shared with Hitler was a fear and hatred of liberals, socialists, and Communists. Yet, like Goering, he had little doubt that the Communists were responsible for the Reichstag conflagration.

That same evening, Paul Joseph Goebbels got word of the fire by phone. Dr. Ernst Hanfstaengl, the Nazi Press Chief, was staying at Goering's Reichstag residence, the palace of the President of the Reichstag. When he heard the noise of fire engines rushing to the Reichstag, he immediately telephoned Goebbels, his superior. But Goebbels thought Hanfstaengl was playing some kind of a trick on him. He said nothing of the call to his guest, Chancellor Hitler.

But then Goebbels had second thoughts, and he returned Hanfstaengl's call.

"Come see for yourself," shouted Hanfstaengl.

Goebbels was still not convinced. He called the police station in the Reichstag district.

"The whole building is burning!" responded the police. Hanfstaengl had not been joking. The music party at the home of the Minister of Propaganda came to an abrupt end. The Fuehrer, Goebbels, and the rest of the party got into their cars and, with a huge escort, raced through the city to the site of the raging fire.

As Hitler himself entered the Reichstag, he met Hermann Goering, who immediately reported his findings — and his opinion — to the Fuehrer.

According to Goering, there could be no doubt that the fire had been started by the Communists. Communist deputies to the Reichstag were the last to leave the building, shortly before the fire was discovered. Indeed, Goering told Hitler, a Communist had been discovered in the burning building and

Dripping hoses drape the ornate lobby of the Reichstag on the day after the fire, as Berlin police and fire officials assess the damage.

arrested. He also notified Hitler that he had ordered a mobilization of all city police and a special guard detailed for every public building in Berlin.

"This is the beginning of a Communist uprising," declared Goering. "But we are ready for anything."

Hitler, who had controlled himself up to now, suddenly went red in the face and started to scream: "Now we'll show them! Anyone who stands in our way will be mown down. The German people have been soft too long. Every Communist official must be shot. All Communist deputies must be hanged this very night. All friends of the Communists must be locked up. And that goes for the Social Democrats as well!"

The Social Democrats were anti-Communist, but anti-Nazi as well. The Iron Front, an organization of armed Social Democrats, was ready to defend the German Republic against any attempted take-over by either of the extremes, right or left. But Hitler would permit neither the Social Democrats nor their armed force to deter his drive for supreme control of the Reich. He would use the Reichstag fire as a pretext to annihilate not only the Communist party, but any opposition to him at all in Germany.

"This is a God-given signal," he shouted to Vice-Chancellor von Papen, whose hand he shook with unusual vigor. "If this fire, as I believe, is the work of Communists, then we must crush this pest with an iron fist!"

The Fuehrer had forgotten the Social Democrats for a moment, but only for a moment. Anything and everything in his path to power was to be met with the "iron fist." Assassination and murder were to become the order of the day in Germany. Nothing and nobody would stop Hitler from his diabolic purpose.

Except for Heinrich Himmler, who was in Munich at the

time, only one important Nazi was not at the Reichstag that night. Wolf von Helldorf, the veteran storm trooper who was destined to be executed as a member of the resistance against Hitler in 1944, had been informed of the fire in one of the taverns he was visiting that evening. The startling news seemed to make no impression on him. Although the man responsible for the safety of Hitler and his party in Berlin, he simply announced that he was tired. He was going home to bed. He did ask his aide to go down to the Reichstag to see what was happening and let him know if there was anything serious to report. That was all.

Such an attitude and such action (or lack of it) on the part of Count von Helldorf might have been considered rather strange, even suspicious. The Communists were to claim that the Nazis themselves had put the torch to the Reichstag for their own propagandistic and political purposes. It was a claim that most people throughout the world came to believe was the truth about the Reichstag fire.

But Hitler was not concerned at the moment with any people outside the German Reich. Nor were any people outside the Reich capable of influencing the turn of events in the German Republic. It was a republic born out of defeat of a mighty German army in World War I. Its life and existence, due largely to the will of a ruthless Hitler, would be short, and it would end in a bloodbath of political and racial murder.

To understand the circumstances that culminated in the Reichstag fire, it is necessary to trace the path Germany took following World War I.

Germany Defeated

In the autumn of 1918 in the fourth year of World War I, German troops occupied conquered territory that stretched from France to Russia's Crimea. But the coalition that Kaiser Wilhelm II had forged in the war against the Allies was rapidly coming apart at the seams. Bulgaria surrendered to the victorious Allied troops in September of 1918. Turkey signed an armistice with the Allies in October. On November 4, 1918, the Austro-Hungarian Empire surrendered. Germany stood alone and, for all its conquests, there was great dissatisfaction among its soldiers at the war fronts and open rebellion within its borders.

In September 1918, General Erich Ludendorff, one of Kaiser Wilhelm's top generals, urged his emperor to form a democratic government in Germany, which would press for the end of the war. Ludendorff was dismissed.

Two weeks later, Field Marshall Paul von Hindenburg urged the Kaiser to abdicate the German throne. On November 10, Kaiser Wilhelm II fled his country, and for the rest of his life lived in Doorn, a small village in Holland.

On November 11, 1918, the Germans and the Allies agreed on a cease-fire — an armistice. Friedrich Ebert, a moderate Socialist, was named the head of a provisional government, and Germany was proclaimed a republic. The seat of the government was the city of Weimar, the same city that Johann Wolfgang von Goethe, the great German poet, had made the center of German culture. The German Republicans thought Weimar would be far enough away from Berlin to escape the pressure of the militarists and the Communists. They proved to be wrong.

Ebert had agreed on the interim government only after General Groener had promised him the support of the German army against Communist or any other threat to the Republic. He also insisted that von Hindenburg continue at the head of the beaten German armed forces. By the same token, Ebert, despite his professed liberal sentiments, agreed to the army's retaining its old power and its elite position in German society.

Whatever the understanding between the provisional president and the generals, it did not really matter for very long. The Weimar Republic was born out of defeat into utter chaos. Eventually it would be betrayed and would be the one to hand it over to Hitler and the Nazis.

Civil War in Postwar Germany

Even before Wilhelm II abdicated and fled to Holland and before the provisional government of the Republic was proclaimed, soldiers and workers in Germany were organizing themselves into Soldiers' and Workers' Councils and assuming power. This is what had happened in Russia on the eve of its revolution. The councils called for the abolition of the regular army and for the dismissal of von Hindenburg from his post. Like the Russian Bolsheviks, the German soldiers and workers demanded complete political control of the country.

Ebert was fully aware of the danger of this movement to the survival of the young German Republic. He was prepared for it. When, on December 23, 1918, the Sparticists (German Communists), under the leadership of Karl Liebknecht and Rosa Luxemberg, attempted a military take-over, Ebert called on the army for the help it had promised him. During the week of January 10, an army of regular troops and the newly formed Free Corps detachments (volunteer anti-Communist ex-soldiers) struck. Rosa Luxemberg and Karl Liebknecht were captured and killed by their captors. The Sparticists were utterly routed.

In November 1918 in Bavaria, one of the larger provinces in South Germany, Kurt Eisner had been president of an independent republic. In April 1919 he was assassinated and a Communist regime took over. In May 1919, the Free Corps entered Munich, the capital of Bavaria, and smashed the Communist government in a bloodbath that took the lives of hundreds of innocent people. Bavaria thus became part of the Weimar Republic. But the actual power in Bavaria was the Free Corps and its reactionary leaders. Munich was to provide the fertile soil from which the Nazi party would spring.

The Versailles Treaty—
Assassination—
Rebellion

Violence became almost a way of life in the very young German Republic. The Communists were by no means destroyed as a force in Germany after the defeat of the Sparticists. But the greater threat and practice of violence came from the right — the old army men, the Free Corps, and the extreme nationalists.

On May 7, 1919, the terms of the Versailles Treaty were published in Berlin. The demands that the victorious Allies expected the Germans to meet were harsh. Germany was stunned and angry.

The Versailles Treaty called for Germany to return the provinces of Alsace and Lorraine to France. (The two provinces had been claimed by both the French and the Germans for many, many years, and the Germans had taken them from the French after the Franco-Prussian War of 1870-1.) The treaty also called for the German surrender of the coal-rich Saar region, the port of Danzig, her entire colonial empire in Africa, and her navy. In addition, Germany was to limit her armed forces to 100,000 men, and her armaments were to be severely curtailed. The Germans would also be required to make huge monetary payments, by way of reparation, to their former enemies.

The answer to the publication of these terms was immediate and vociferous protest on the part of the German people. They demanded that the war be resumed, that the army go back to its fighting.

The Germans are a proud people, and their pride has been well nourished. After centuries of disunity the separate German states had at last become a united nation after the Franco-Prus-

February 1919. Friedrich Ebert (center) is proclaimed head of the new German Republic. He is shown here leaving the National Assembly at Weimar, seat of the new postwar government.

sian War, with the brilliant statesman Otto von Bismarck as its leader. In the brief forty-four years of its existence up to 1914, Germany had become a world power. Georg Hegel, the great German philosopher of the nineteenth century, had told the German people that true reason resided in the German state. The people had been told endlessly by politicians, generals, and writers that the Germany that had produced the greatest philosophers, the greatest music, the greatest scientists, writers, and artists was the greatest country in Europe — indeed in the world — and it must be victorious.

The Germans could not accept the humiliating defeat thrust on them by the Versailles Treaty. Nor could they countenance the dismemberment of their fatherland. Phillipp Scheidemann, Chancellor of the Weimar Republic, shouted: "May the hand wither that signs this treaty!" His words were echoed in demonstrations in many cities and towns of the young and insecure Republic.

Once more, Ebert turned to his generals for advice. Should he sign or not sign? Of all the German people, there were none prouder than its professional army officers, but they knew, better than most, that there was no choice in the matter. The war-weary German armies, they reported to Ebert, were in no position to defend the country against a renewed attack from the West. Ebert had only one way to go. He signed the treaty. The reaction throughout Germany resulted in a wave of political assassinations.

Matthias Erzberger, leader of the Catholic Center party, was shot down while taking a walk. Foreign Minister Walter Rathenau was shot from a car speeding by. From 1918 through 1922, there were at least 376 political murders in Germany. The radical left was responsible for 22 assassinations, the radical right for 354. And in all that time, only 62 of those accused of assassination were convicted of murder. Ten of the 62 were condemned to death. All ten of those given the death sentence were members of left-wing groups. Ebert, or his judges, either shut their eyes to, or underestimated the danger to, the Republic from the right-wing extremists. And it was a right-wing extremist who would ultimately destroy the Weimar Republic.

It was a right-wing extremist named Gustav von Kahr who ousted the Socialist government in Munich in 1920 and took over. Munich was by this time the haven for all anti-Republican forces, for those who aimed to tear up the Versailles Treaty, for anti-Semitism, and for the growing National Socialist (Nazi) party.

It was in March of that same year, 1920, that the Free Corps struck at the heart of the Republic. Led by Walther von Luettewitz, the general who had ruthlessly and efficiently destroyed the Sparticist threat to the Ebert government, the Free Corps took over Berlin, as the regular army (the Reichswehr) stood by and watched. Ebert fled. Wolfgang Kapp, a politician of the extreme right, was declared Chancellor.

This time it was the working people of Berlin who saved the Republic. They declared a general strike. The city was paralyzed. It was Kapp's turn to flee from the capital.

Ebert returned to his office, but he knew that his government rested on very insecure ground. There were irreconcilable differences between the many different political groups in Germany, between Monarchists and Democrats, Socialists and Communists, Communists and Conservatives, Republicans and anti-Republicans. There were class differences, too, between military men and businessmen, between the royalist elite and the common people, between capital and labor. Nor could Ebert rid the government of the antagonism created by his signing the Versailles Treaty. Certainly it was Ebert's desire for peace

A machine gunner stands guard during the Kapp putsch of 1920 in Berlin. Putsch nearly succeeded as dissatisfied army elements and right-wingers gained control of the city for several days.

and unity that governed the punishment he meted out to the perpetrators of the abortive putsch. Only one man, a Berlin policeman, was convicted for the crime of rebellion. His sentence was an almost apologetic five years of "honorary confinement."

Yet the right-wing extremists, despite their failure in Berlin, would not be deterred in their efforts to topple the Republic. Just beginning to seriously spearhead that effort was the National Socialist party.

The Beginnings
of the Nazi Party

Immediately following Germany's defeat in 1918 and the creation of the German Republic, and particularly after the signing of the Versailles Treaty, many small anti-Republican groups were independently organized all over Germany. This was especially true in Munich, the hotbed of anti-Republican activity. Most of these groups, for lack of money or public support or internal bickering, died quickly. However, one such group in Munich, the German Workers' party, managed to survive and afterward to flourish.

A young war veteran named Adolf Hitler, who had been making right-wing speeches for the army, was sent by his superiors to investigate this minute organization of little more than fifty members. The army suspected that it might be Communist. Nothing could have been further from fact. The German Workers' party, created in 1919, met in the backroom of one or another of the many taverns in Munich to deliver long anti-Republican speeches to one another and to expound crackpot theories and solutions for Germany's economic problems. They attacked communism and the Communists, demanded that Germany tear up the Versailles Treaty, and harangued against the Jews. Outside their tavern meetings, their principal activity consisted of harassing and beating up any Jews they came across.

One of the leading members of this verbose German Workers' party was reputed to be a mediocre poet who drank too much. Another was a mentally confused locksmith. A third was a "doctor" who entertained strange political theories. Still another was an engineer with curious economic concepts. Ernst Roehm, a professional soldier, would be the only one of this grotesque group to leave a mark on German history — a very ugly mark.

Roehm was a captain in the German Regular Army. He had lost the upper part of his nose in the first year of World War I. He was a hard man and a ruthless one. He would build the sadistic, brutal, illegal army for the National Socialist party (Nazi) and for his future Fuehrer, Adolf Hitler.

Hitler, as his army superiors had ordered, sat in on one of the meetings of this ludicrous group of misfits and was evidently impressed by what he saw and heard. Perhaps it was the possibilities he saw in the group that impressed him. In any case, it did not take him long to join them. In 1919, he became the fifty-fifth member of the German Workers' party.

But Hitler was not just a joiner. Nervous, intense, he immediately began to put all his efforts into recruiting and building up the ranks of his party. Very quickly he became its chief propagandist, its principal speaker, a rabble-rouser.

It was not long before the backrooms of the Munich taverns became too small to hold the membership and the mass meetings of the German Workers' party. They began to hire bigger halls to seat the larger and larger crowds Hitler drew to their advertised rallies. And the larger the audience he drew, the more power Hitler demanded in making party policy and decisions, and the more he took.

Hitler changed the name of the German Workers' party to the National Socialist German Workers' party, which in German was abbreviated to Nazi. He gave the party its own flag, with the hooked cross, the swastika, as its insignia. He organized a group of disaffected and anti-Republican war veterans into a

Captain Ernst Roehm, pictured here several years before he became head of Hitler's Storm Troopers (S.A.).

26

Mass demonstration outside the Reichstag by Communist organizations and other groups in 1920. Soon Hitler's Nazi troopers were able to break up these and other rival gatherings.

notorious strong-arm squad and put them into brown uniforms. They were called the Sturmabteilung, or S.A. At first the job of the S.A. was to keep order at Nazi rallies and meetings, to get rid of any heckler who dared to raise his voice. The duties of the S.A., however, expanded quickly. Sometimes with Ernst Roehm at their head, sometimes Hitler, they raided and broke up meetings and rallies of Communists, Social Democrats, any other of their many rival parties. They also intensified their harassment of the Jewish population of Munich.

In the summer of 1921, a significant number of the membership of the National Socialist German Workers' party was of the opinion that Hitler had assumed too much power in their ranks. They tried to take some of this authority away from him and clamp down on his growing dictatorial practices. But they failed.

Beating down all opposition and forcing his will on his colleagues, Adolf Hitler became the undisputed leader of the National Socialist German Workers' party in the summer of 1921.

The Nazi Party Grows

At first the influence of Hitler and his party was limited to Munich and Bavaria. That influence would continue to increase. Soon its power would be heard and felt throughout the turbulent and unhappy German Republic.

Alfred Rosenberg, who would prove to be an important diplomatic figure in Hitler's Third Reich, came to Munich and joined forces with the Fuehrer. Rudolf Hess had been with Hitler almost from the beginning. In Munich and after, he developed a doglike devotion to his leader. Another to join Hitler in Munich was one of the heroes of the Baron von Richthofen Flying Squadron of World War I, Hermann Goering. Goering was also generous with the money he contributed to the Nazi cause. Ernst Hanfstaengl, a man who had been graduated from Harvard University, was another to give a considerable amount of money to the Nazi treasury.

Such funds provided arms and uniforms for the military squads that the Nazis organized. It also supplied the means for spreading their propaganda throughout the Reich, a Reich that was increasingly ready, willing, and even eager to accept the kind of demagoguery Hitler and his party spewed out.

Defeated and humiliated, the German people sought some path that would return them their dignity, the pride that they had been nourished on before the collapse of the German Empire in the war with the Allies. Hitler showed them a way.

He preached the superiority of the German people. More precisely, he preached the superiority of the Nordic race. It was a thesis that every anthropologist of merit scorned as a perversion of fact, but it was a thesis that a good segment of the German population accepted. The true Nordic German, Hitler ranted, was pure, innocent, and strong. It was the impure, the decadent, the corrupt, shouted the Fuehrer, who were responsible for Germany's defeat in battle and its humiliation. And the Jew, according to Hitler's stentorian argument, was that impurity in the midst of the German people. It was the Jew, for Hitler, who had brought Germany down to defeat and humiliation.

What was more, international communism was equated with international banking, and international banking with the Jew. Truth and facts were never important to Hitler. But the "big lie," he discovered quite early, could prove a mighty weapon. He used it and used it well. And many Germans, desperately eager for a return of their honor and dignity, did not stop to question, did not stop to test or evaluate, the ravings of the Fuehrer. Like a dry land that greedily drinks up a sudden rain, they swallowed the evil propaganda, the half-truths, and the big lies. They did not know that Hitler's "final solution" would in time take the lives of six million Jews and others in the gas chambers, concentration camps, and extermination camps of Majdanek, Treblinka, Oswiecim, Dachau, Belsen, Buchenwald, and others. But these horrors were yet to come, and many Germans, with no inkling of the terrible days ahead, flocked to the banners and the malevolent Hitler and his cohorts.

The weaknesses of the German Republic, under the leadership of the moderate Socialist Friedrich Ebert, made the recruiting and the work of the Fuehrer that much easier. The defeated army and its general staff, curtailed by the Versailles Treaty, had promised to support Ebert. Ebert, in turn, had promised to maintain the status and power of the elite General Staff. But both were openly defied by anti-Republican forces of both the right and the left, and by the pro-Republican forces as well. The law of the land had little meaning and less respect in the postwar chaos of Germany, and there was precious little evidence indeed of what might be called order in the country.

The Social Democrats had their own private armed force, the Iron Front. The Nazis had their S.A. In addition roving bands of war veterans, calling themselves the Free Corps, moved about independently or attached themselves to one anti-Republican force or another. As for the Communists, they too had their armed bands. Each political organization in Germany had its fighting men who were well-equipped with weapons and ready to attack or defend themselves against the others. There were street battles and shooting. The police and the regular army just looked on, or moved away to some safer location. They did little or nothing to stop the pitched battles between rival political groups.

When a government cannot keep peace and order among its citizens, it has little control over the country's economy. Germany, which lost considerable valuable land and now had to pay huge sums of money in war indemnities, was faced with the severest kind of economic crisis. Ebert's government was unable to cope with it.

In 1920, an American dollar was worth 20 German marks. In 1921, the same dollar was worth 75 marks and by 1922, 400 marks. With the rapidly declining value of the mark went a rapidly declining ability of the German people to import essential raw and finished goods. Mounting inflation in Germany elevated the price of meat, groceries, and services. And the situation was going to get much worse.

By 1923, the American dollar was worth 7,000 marks. The German government was producing the paper mark at a quicker and quicker pace, but it was fast becoming nothing more than worthless paper. Shops began to shut their doors. Mills began to close down. There was no profit in production, no profit in sales. With the closing of the shops and mills, there was less and less work. Unemployment and hunger took over.

And the unemployed and the hungry moved into the ranks of the Nazis. Demagoguery feeds unemployment, hunger, misery; and Hitler was a master at turning the unhappiness of his people to his own advantage.

Germany, in its dismal economic condition, asked the Allies for more time in which to pay the indemnities due them. France rejected the request. When the Germans failed to make a due payment to the French, France sent troops into Germany's Ruhr Valley. The region of the Ruhr was the most essential factor in Germany's economy. The Ruhr provided the Reich with 80 percent of its coal and steel. The French move may not have stopped production in that area, but it was the ultimate in the humiliation of the German people.

The workers resisted. They refused to work the mines or the steel mills. There was some sabotage and some guerrilla warfare. The French retaliated with force. They made mass arrests. They expelled large numbers of Germans from the territory. Some Germans were even tried for one crime or another, convicted, and executed.

Eventually, the men went back to work the mines and the mills, and the French withdrew their troops. But the damage had been done. In six months the mark had plummeted to a new low. A dollar could now be exchanged for 18,000 marks. Five months later, it would be worth 4 billion marks.

The salary of the German worker was worth nothing in the market or at the grocery store. The money in the banks that people had invested in German industry was worthless, too. Whatever confidence the German people may have had in their government was now gone. The government that had urged them to save and to invest in the economy of the Reich

When Germany could not pay reparation payments due according to the Versailles Treaty, French troops occupied such Ruhr cities as Essen. Here French troops guard a post office. Such scenes added greatly to the Germans' national humiliation.

had defaulted on all its promises. The German people felt that they had been bilked and robbed. Germany was bankrupt, and the ranks of Hitler's Nazi party swelled with recruits, recruits eager to put Germany back on its economic feet again and certain that Hitler was the man to do it.

The Beer-Hall Putsch
of 1923

The French occupation of the Ruhr had triggered a number
of armed rebellions in the Reich. Major Buchrucker, once a
member of the German General Staff, mobilized the Black
Reichswehr, an illegal armed force, and occupied a few government buildings in Berlin and briefly the Spandau citadel. But
that was as far as he got. He went down to defeat under the
attack of the regular army under General Hans von Seeckt.
The general also suppressed Communist uprisings in Hamburg,
Thuringia, Saxony, and the Ruhr. Bavaria, however, presented
a more difficult problem.

Gustav von Kahr, a monarchist; Otto von Lossow, com-
mander of the Bavarian Reichswehr; and Colonel Hans von
Seisser, chief of police, had taken over the government in
Munich. There was talk and agitation for secession from the
Reich. The triumvirate, with absolute dictatorial power in Ba-
varia, refused to take orders from Berlin.

Von Seeckt again came to the fore. He sent word to Munich that he would not countenance their rebellious action.
He indicated that if necessary he was ready to march his army
into Bavaria in order to maintain German law in that province.

Kahr, Lossow, and Seisser became nervous. They began
to waver in their determination to free Bavaria from the rule
of Berlin. But Hitler, who had also received warning from von
Seeckt, stood firm. More than that, with his own party pressur-
ing him, he decided on a plan to abduct the ruling triumvirate
and to compel them to act as he willed. Only the knowledge
that his own armies were not yet strong enough for the task
stopped Hitler from immediately taking over the government
of Bavaria.

There was a German Memorial Day parade scheduled for November 4, 1923, and it was to be reviewed by Munich's ruling trio. Hitler's plan was to move in a mass of his storm troopers armed with machine guns to isolate and make prisoners of the triumvirate. That done, he intended to proclaim a Bavarian revolution and, at gun point, force Kahr, Lossow, and Seisser to endorse his action.

Two circumstances put an end to this wild plan. First, Hitler discovered that the route of the march would be along very narrow streets, which would cramp the movement of his own troops. Second, the streets were going to be unusually well guarded by an exceptionally large contingent of Munich police. There had to be some other way to carry out his plans.

Next Hitler planned a complete take-over of the city by force. On the night of November 10-11, his fully-armed henchmen would seize every important building and square in Munich. If this could be accomplished, Hitler reasoned that the triumvirate would have no choice but to follow his dictates. This was another plan that was never carried out because a a simpler alternative suddenly presented itself.

On the 8th of November, a huge business meeting was scheduled to take place in the Buergerbräukeller, a large beer hall in Munich. Kahr, Lossow, and Seisser were scheduled to attend. Here was a comparatively small area in which Hitler's storm troopers could act with speed, full strength, and efficiency.

Hitler waited until the beer hall was full. He had surrounded it with his swastika-badged army, their rifles ready, their machine guns mounted. Then, in his most theatrical fashion, he burst through the doors of the large hall, jumped up onto one of the tables, and fired a shot from his pistol up into the ceiling.

"The National Revolution has begun!" he shouted to a

stunned audience. "The barracks of the Reichswehr and police are occupied! The army and the police are marching on the city under the swastika banner!"

This was not true. Hitler was bluffing. But no one in the beer hall dared call him a liar.

At gun point, he forced Kahr, Lossow, and Seisser into a side room. Here, he demanded that they join him in the rebellion, or *putsch*. The triumvirate protested but the gun proved a persuasive argument, and Hitler ran back into the main hall of the tavern to announce that he and the triumvirate were creating a new national government. The response of the crowd was noisy and joyous, and their shouting could be heard in the room where the triumvirate were virtually prisoners.

Now General Erich Ludendorff entered the hall, escorted by Hitler's troops. A brilliant strategist, Ludendorff had been a World War I hero. He was also violently anti-Republican. While he was annoyed that a mere corporal (Hitler) should presume to put himself on a par with a general, he could not resist the role Hitler had made possible for him. He urged a friendship between Hitler and the triumvirate and his urging seemed to have its effect. One after another, each one of the trio faced the beer-hall mob and pledged loyalty to each other and to the newborn political setup.

But not too far away there was trouble at the barracks of the Regular Army Engineers. The regulars and the storm troopers had come face to face and the confrontation threatened to develop into an armed conflict between the two opposing forces. Hitler, informed of the dangerous situation, abruptly left the hall to restore peace between the two antagonistic elements. He wanted the army with him, not against him.

While Hitler did manage to stop the threat of shooting at the barracks, he paid a price for it. When he got back to the beer hall, his triumvirate had vanished. They had simply walked out of the hall. And they were nowhere to be found in the city. They had left and gone into hiding. The beer-hall putsch had collapsed.

It was General Ludendorff who suggested to a troubled Hitler one last attempt to take over Bavaria in 1923. With a variation of Hitler's own plan for seizing Munich, Ludendorff recommended a march to the center of town in broad daylight. The Fuehrer was not too enamored of this tactic suggested by the old general, but there was nothing he could think of in its place. Thus he put the plan into motion.

At about noon on November 9, 1923, the Fuehrer, with General Ludendorff at his side, marched about 3,000 storm troopers toward their objective. The Fuehrer carried a revolver. His men were armed with rifles and machine guns. At the Ludwig Bridge the parade was stopped by several armed policemen.

Hermann Goering and Rudolf Hess, who were marching side by side with Hitler, threatend to shoot it out if their own men were not allowed to pass. The police, vastly outnumbered by the Nazis, withdrew from their posts and Hitler's troops marched on.

They moved into Marienplatz and toward the War Ministry. Here Ernst Roehm, leader of the storm troopers, and a portion of his men were surrounded and held at bay by a detachment of regular army soldiers.

Hitler and the rest of his troops had moved into the Residenzstrasse. This was a narrow street in which about 100 armed police officers were waiting for them.

Again, Goering tried to talk his way through, but this time the police did not budge. There was a gunshot. It was like a signal. Both sides of the street began to fire.

Goering was wounded. Sixteen Nazis were killed. So were three policemen. Many more were wounded. The two men at Hitler's side, who had been marching in close formation with their arms interlocked, were hit and fell. Hitler fell with them, a bone in his shoulder broken. Of the whole contingent of some 3,000 Nazis and their sympathizers, only Ludendorff marched on down that narrow street, as only a Prussian general could.

But the attempted Nazi putsch had failed. Goering fled to Austria. Roehm surrendered. Hitler was clapped into jail. It was not, however, the end of Hitler and his National Socialist party.

The Fuehrer was tried for treason, convicted, and sentenced to five years of imprisonment in the old fortress of Landsberg. But he was eligible for parole in six months and actually released in less than nine. Yet he made those nine months memorable by writing *Mein Kampf* ("My Struggle"), the book in which he outlined the essential strategy for his future conquests.

Young Adolf Hitler is photographed here with General Erich Ludendorff at the time of the beer-hall putsch in Munich.

A Change in Fortune
for Germany

When Hitler was released from Landsberg just before Christmas, 1924, he discovered that his party had undergone a considerable change. Some of his most trusted aides had disappeared into the countryside or had left Germany altogether. There was considerable bickering in the ranks and open rivalry in the top echelon. The Nazis were, in fact, no longer the solid organization they had been before Hitler was jailed. In fact, there was a strong tendency among the membership to disband and dissolve the party entirely.

There was good reason for all of this. Greater than the change that had taken place in the National Socialist party was the change beginning to take shape in all of Germany.

Thanks largely to the financial genius of Dr. Hjalmar Schacht, president of the Reichsbank, Germany was to experience an abrupt and dramatic economic recovery. With the help of huge loans from the United States, the Germans were able to meet their reparations debts to the Allies. They were able to stabilize the value of the mark. The wheels of industry began to turn once more, the shops to open their doors. The massive unemployment figures decreased. By 1928 there was almost full employment in Germany, and the Republic had become one of the most prosperous countries in Europe.

From 1920 to 1925, Hitler had been able to draw hundreds of thousands of his followers from among the unemployed, the bankrupt, and both the hungry working class and middle class.

A determined Adolf Hitler is shown here leaving the Landsberg prison in December 1924. He used the few months he spent there to write his famous Mein Kampf.

From 1925 to 1929, though the Nazis continued to grow, the working people, the shopkeepers, the small merchants, all were too busy at their jobs, at their trades, in their stores, too busy enjoying the general prosperity to pay much attention to the man who would radically alter the structure of their country.

Friedrich Ebert had died in 1925. Paul von Hindenburg, a traditionalist and conservative, had been elected President of the Republic. Above all else, he represented stability. This was what the German people wanted in those good years from 1925 to 1929. They did not want Hitler, the Nazis, or anyone else to upset the full applecart.

But this happy change in fortune for the people of Germany was not going to last. Just as the economic tides had turned abruptly in their favor, the tides would turn again and plunge the country into deeper despair.

On October 28-29, 1929, the New York Stock Exchange was a scene of utter bedlam. The market crashed with reverberations that were felt all around the world. It heralded perhaps the deepest and longest financial and economic depression in all history.

Loans to Germany from the United States dried up. Factories and mills shut their doors throughout the world. Millions of stores and small businesses went bankrupt. So did hundreds and hundreds of banks. Germany, like every other country, suffered too. Perhaps Germany, still with an enormous war debt, suffered more and more quickly than most.

Again the wheels of German industry ground down to a halt, or close to it. Again the shopkeepers closed and locked their doors. Again the people of Germany were hungry. Six million were unemployed, 14.2 percent of the German work force. Later the unemployment would reach 20 percent of the work force. The devastating nature of this situation may be measured

A one-billion-mark note, worth next to nothing in Berlin during the late 1920s. The collapse of the German economy greatly aided the Nazi rise to power.

against the drastic situation at that time in the United States, when 12.5 percent of its working people were without jobs.

Bad times lend themselves to agitation, rebellion, revolution. There were riots in every major city in Germany. There were armed conflicts, fighting, pitched battles in the streets. Once more the Republic had failed its people and the extremes of both left and right rediscovered their voices and flexed their muscles.

Adolf Hitler, who had quietly been building his forces, was prepared for this unhappy moment in the life of the troubled Republic. He took full advantage of the miseries of its people. Like an ugly rash, his banners and storm troopers began to flood the streets, brazenly parading their strength. And many discontented men, women, and even children of Germany were swept into his ranks by his satanic oratory and demagoguery.

Thousands took up the banner of the swastika and swelled the numbers of the National Socialist party. This time, Hitler would prevail.

The Phenomenal Growth
of the Nazis

In 1925 the membership of the National Socialist party totaled no more than 27,000. A persistent campaign increased its ranks to 49,000 by 1926. In 1927, there were 72,000 Nazis and in 1928, despite the country's prosperity, 108,000.

With the first signs of the depression the number of followers jumped to 178,000. After 1929, with the economy of Germany moving rapidly toward complete collapse, the growth of the National Socialist party became phenomenal.

In 1928, the Nazis polled less than 3 percent of the country's vote in its national election of delegates to the Riechstag. They were able to win only 12 of the 600 seats and were ninth in rank, the weakest party in the German national legislature.

In 1930, however, the results of the general election were dramatically different. The depression and Hitler's demagoguery combined to produce a seed that grew to a frightening harvest. A total of 6,409,600 Germans cast their votes for the National Socialist party candidates. In just two years, the Nazis had increased their voting strength by approximately 800 percent and they captured 107 seats in the Reichstag. The National Socialist party was now the second-largest and strongest party in the Reichstag. Hitler was well on the way to his avowed goal: complete control of the Reich and of the German people. He had organized well for it.

In 1930, his private army numbered 100,000. They were the S.A. — the well-armed, brown-shirted Sturmabteilung (Storm Division) — and the S.S. — the black-uniformed Schutzstaffel (Defense Corps). By January of 1932, their numbers had increased to 400,000. In huge groups they moved into the streets, with their swastika emblems prominent. They

Nuremberg, 1929. Adolf Hitler, decked out in brown-shirt uniform, salutes his storm troopers.

sought out all enemies of Hitler, real or imagined. They harassed, destroyed, and murdered. They were armed to fight, and they looked for fights and found them.

They were a blustering, brutal army, and they claimed control of the streets wherever they marched. But often enough their claim was challenged, particularly by the armed forces of the German Communist party.

Hundreds of pitched battles were fought in the streets. In one three-week period in Prussia alone, there were more than 460 such pitched battles. In June and July of 1932, again in Prussia, almost 200 people were killed in street fighting and almost 700 people were wounded. The opposition fought valiantly, but the sheer numbers of the Nazis and their arms gave them an unbeatable advantage. And, there was another advantage that they were going to take for themselves in very short order.

Another Kind of Activity in the Weimar Republic

The story of the Weimar Republic of Germany was not entirely one of turmoil and strife. In its short life, the Republic was also a witness to a remarkable outburst of creative energies in arts and letters, architecture, theater, motion pictures, and in the sciences. Thomas Mann wrote his famous *Magic Mountain* despite the country's chaos. Stefan Zweig and Lion Feuchtwanger, among others, were writing other important novels. Bertolt Brecht wrote poetry and plays that continue to be produced all over the world; Kurt Weill was writing great music; and Alban Berg wrote his famous opera *Wozzeck*. Walter Gropius established his influential school of architecture, the Bauhaus, and Max Beckmann, among other artists, painted significant works of art. There was also Max Reinhardt in the theater and there were many important motion picture productions. In the sciences, Sigmund Freud continued his work in psychiatry, Albert Einstein his labors in abstract mathematics, and there were a number of brilliant German scientists working in nuclear physics.

With the ascendency of Hitler most of them were to flee Germany. For Hitler, except for the scientists, the cultural product of the Weimar Republic was dangerously cosmopolitan, corrupt, Jewish. It was a culture he destroyed when he came to power.

50

Hitler Heads
the Reichstag

In the July 1932 national elections in Germany, the Nazis emerged with their greatest strength in the national legislature. Within the short space of only a few months, they practically doubled their popular vote and more than doubled their number of deputies in the Reichstag. As many as 13,745,000 Germans cast their ballots for the swastika and 230 Nazis were elected deputies to the German parliament.

Hitler still lacked a clear-cut majority in the 608-seat Reichstag, but the National Socialist party was clearly the number-one party in Germany. Hitler expected the aging President of the Republic, Paul von Hindenburg, to name him Chancellor, a post equivalent to that of Prime Minister in England and the top political office in the country. Von Hindenburg had other ideas.

The old general, a Prussian career officer, could not countenance a mere corporal, and a foreigner to boot, as head of the government. Hitler had been no more than a low-ranking noncommissioned officer in the German army during the war, and he had been born in Austria. Indirectly, von Hindenburg did offer Hitler the Vice-Chancellor position in the German cabinet, but no more.

Hitler raged. His storm troopers urged that he take over the government by force. But von Hindenburg would not be moved by "the corporal's" anger, nor by the threat of his private armed forces.

For all his raving and ranting, Hitler insisted on the "legal" process. He was determined that von Hindenburg would yet name him Chancellor. He kept his storm troopers in order, and managed to get the Reichstag dissolved for still another election

Despite mutual dislike of each other, Adolf Hitler and President von Hindenburg occasionally greeted one another in public, as here in Berlin. Note black-uniformed S.S. troops giving Nazi salute in background.

in 1932. He was sure that this time his party could win enough seats in the Reichstag to give the Nazis an undisputed majority. An absolute majority would force the hand of von Hindenburg. The old general would then have no other choice than to give the Fuehrer the political office he wanted.

Hitler was headed for a disappointment. For the first time, the Nazi tide was reversed. The National Socialists lost two million votes in the November 1932 elections. They lost 34 seats in the Reichstag. The Nazis now had only 196 deputies in the German parliament. However, it was still the largest single bloc in the legislature and Hitler made good use of it.

Again he was offered a place in the Reichstag cabinet, but not the chancellorship itself. Again he refused. Hitler also saw to it that no one else Hindenburg appointed to that office could operate efficiently or create a stable and workable government. His huge bloc of votes in the Reichstag made sure of it.

Von Hindenburg tried. Franz von Papen, the professional politician, tried. General Kurt von Schleicher, who had fought on the Russian front in World War I, tried. All attempted rule by decree, without a parliament. All failed.

On January 30, 1933, von Hindenburg gave up the struggle. He called Hitler to his offices and appointed him Chancellor of Germany.

Prelude to the Fire

On becoming Chancellor, Hitler had the Reichstag dissolved and new elections were called for March 5, 1933. He meant to achieve that absolute majority in the German parliament. It was a majority necessary to his ultimate aims.

Hermann Goering, Hitler's Minister of the Interior, helped to insure the victory Hitler wanted. He immediately removed from office hundreds of officials with any kind of pro-Republican sentiment. He replaced them with men whose loyalty to Hitler was assured. Most of these men were members of the S.A. and S.S. He commanded the police to keep their hands off this private army of Hitler's. This gave the storm troopers a free hand and they could now brutalize, destroy, and murder at will.

The Minister of the Interior also ordered the police to use their guns to shoot down anyone who showed any opposition to the government. The government, of course, was Hitler. Goering threatened to punish any police officer who failed to carry out his orders enthusiastically. Toward the end of that year, he had added an extra 50,000 men to his police force, as auxiliaries, to carry out his wishes. Of these men, 40,000 were recruited from the S.S. and the S.A. Most German people were almost completely cowed by roving hordes of thugs.

The purpose of these maneuvers was, of course, to stifle any opposition to the Nazis in the coming March 5th election. The German Communists were forbidden any public meetings of any kind by government (Hitler's) decree. Hitler also shut down the Communist press.

Social Democrat rallies, too, were banned, or else broken up by the S.A. and the S.S. Their newspapers were suspended from time to time at the will of the Fuehrer. The meetings of the Catholic Center party were invaded and dispersed by attack-

Smiling triumphantly, Hitler emerges from ceremonies swearing him in as German Chancellor.

ing storm troopers, and as important a man as Adam Steger-wald, leader of the Catholic Trade Unions, was brutally beaten. There were fifty-one known opponents of Hitler who were murdered by his storm troopers in this pre-election period. The actual count of how many lost their lives at the hands of the Nazis is unknown.

All this was still not enough for Hitler. He had hoped to arouse a rebellion in some quarter of his opposition. Primarily, he had hoped to get a Communist uprising. An open rebellion would give him the excuse to seize power at once and dispense with the legal election. But the uprising did not come. If he could not get the rebellion he wanted, however, he would create the threat of such an uprising. Thus, on February 24, just nine days before the general election, Goering ordered a police raid on the Karl Liebknecht Haus. This was the headquarters of the German Communist party. The police were to collect evidence of a Communist plot to rise up against the government in armed rebellion, and to take over the Reich.

But the Communists, with the rising Nazi terror and the obvious danger to their persons, had vacated the Karl Liebknecht Haus weeks before. Certainly they had taken any documents of importance away with them. However, they did leave a large store of Communist propaganda in the form of leaflets and pamphlets in the cellar of the house. This is what Goering's police seized. And Goering, who was never one to worry about the truth, immediately announced to the press that he had uncovered the Communist blueprint for revolution and that he

As the 1930s progressed, more young men such as these flocked to the Nazi banner. Here, at a national holiday in Nuremberg, Hitler (in car, standing) returns salute, as a smiling Hermann Goering looks on.

had the documents to prove it. He never produced those documents.

If Goering's raid and pronouncement were intended to rush the German people to give overwhelming support to the Nazis, the strategy did not work. Neither the raid nor his speech to the press was met with anything more than mild approval. Of course, anyone who did not approve of Goering's moves and speeches kept his opinion to himself if he valued his life at all. The Nazis needed something more dramatic for their diabolic purposes. They got it just three days after the raid on the Karl Liebknecht Haus — the Reichstag fire!

The Accused and
the Accusers

The fire in the Reichstag gutted the Sessions Chamber, where the deputies met to conduct their legislative business. The firemen had worked earnestly at their task, but the fire had spread with extraordinary speed. There was scarcely any part of the building that had not suffered fire damage. The Reichstag, for all practical purposes, was destroyed. Yet this would matter little to Hitler and his grand design. What was important was that he had been handed a seemingly perfect pretext for his assumption of complete power in Germany.

When the police broke into the burning building, Marinus van der Lubbe of Leyden, Holland, was the only man found in the Reichstag. But the Nazis seemed to have a pre-dated story to explain the conflagration and to implicate their enemies in the arson.

The morning after the fire, they issued a statement in which they accused the Communist party of setting the Reichstag on fire as "the signal for a bloody insurrection and civil war." It was to be only one of the many fires the Communists would set in "government buildings, museums, mansions and essential plants."

The Communists in turn accused the Nazis of starting the blaze for their own propagandistic purposes. They pointed to the underground passageway between the Reichstag and Hermann Goering's residence, as President of the Reichstag. Of course, the Communists did not have the German media, as the Nazis did, to press their accusation that van der Lubbe had been used by the Nazis as a scapegoat for their treacherous action.

Yet both Communists and Nazis were agreed on one point.

59

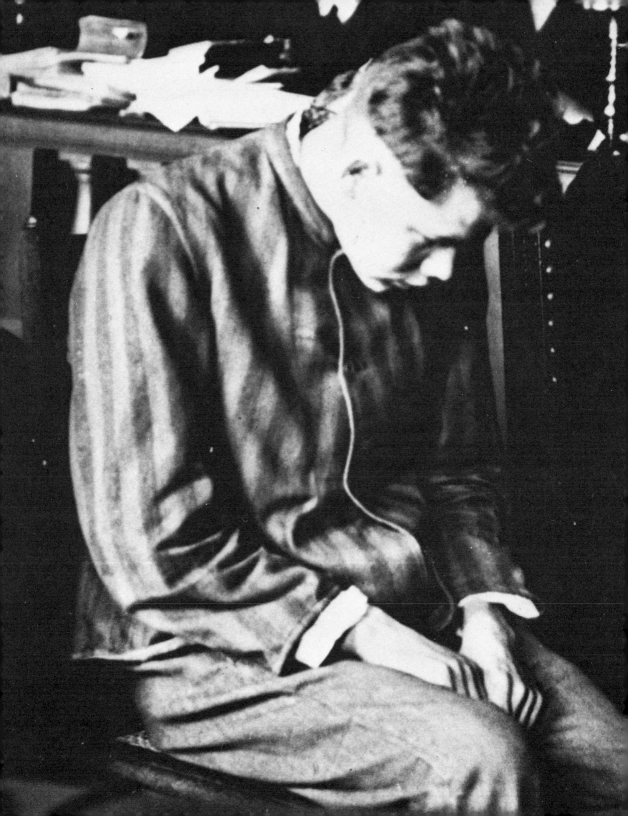

The Reichstag fire was not the work of one man, van der Lubbe. The fire had spread too rapidly for that, they proclaimed. The curtains and the wood had been treated in advance with some highly inflammable chemicals to make them burn quickly. At least, that was the argument from each of the accusers.

When he had been apprehended in the burning Reichstag, van der Lubbe had declared that he alone was responsible for the arson. "Something had to be done in protest against the system," he told the police later. "Since the workers would do nothing, I had to do something myself."

On the Saturday before the Reichstag fire, van der Lubbe admitted he had started three smaller fires — a minor blaze at the Neukolln Welfare Office, another at the Town Hall, and the third at the Imperial Palace. None of these fires was of a serious nature. He insisted, to the very end of his days, that he alone had put the torch to the Reichstag.

Very few would believe van der Lubbe. He was called intelligent, strong-willed, and self-confident by medical experts; but those experts made their testimony in a Nazi-dominated court and may themselves have been Nazis. Goering himself testified that van der Lubbe was half-crazy. And M. François-Poncet, the French Ambassador to Germany who witnessed the trial of van der Lubbe, called the Hollander "feeble-minded, mentally deficient, and probably [the] drugged tool of the real criminals."

Among the "real criminals" whom Goering named was Ernst Torgler, head of the Communist deputies to the Reichstag. The order went out for his arrest on the night of the fire, but he could not be found. Torgler himself went to the police

The accused arsonist Marinus van der Lubbe of Holland, who was found in the Reichstag during the fire.

61

the following morning to protest Goering's order. He was arrested on the spot and clapped into jail.

There were three other Communists accused of complicity in the arson and they also were arrested. One was Georgi Dimitrov, a Bulgarian Communist and the leader of the Central European section of the Communist International. However, the Nazis were not aware of his importance to the international Communist movement. The other two were also Bulgarians, Simon Popov and Vasili Tanev. Along with van der Lubbe, they were accused of the arson and they joined Dimitrov and Torgler in prison.

Actually, these persons were among the more fortunate anti-Nazis — for the moment anyway. They were temporarily safe from the mayhem the forces of Hitler visited on the German people throughout the country. The Nazi reign of terror had begun in earnest.

Storm troopers by the hundreds stormed through the streets of practically every German city, town, and village, breaking into shops and private homes and at all hours of the day and night. They carted off their victims by the truckload, hurled them into their storm-trooper barracks, beat them, tortured them, maimed them, and sometimes killed them. They arrested nearly four thousand Communist officials and anyone else suspected of Communist sympathy. They also arrested leading Social Democrats and others whom they thought might have any liberal leanings, any Republican loyalty, or anti-Nazi sentiment. It is likely that in such a broad and violent attack that any number of Nazi sympathizers suffered along with the rest. Such mass violence lends itself very easily to the settling of private

The German Communist leader Ernst Torgler answers his accusers at the trial.

62

grievance and personal enmity. There was no one to do any checking, and no one to stop the terror. The woods and the rivers concealed the countless corpses of the inhuman savagery. Hitler's storm troopers were in complete command.

Now Hitler had what he wanted. The Reichstag fire had served his purpose. The morning after the arson, he had had von Hindenburg sign a decree placing strict limits on personal freedom, the right of free speech, freedom of association, secrecy of the mails, telegraphs, and telephones. There were to be no restrictions governing house search and confiscation of property. There were no safeguards at all now where the lives and possessions of the German people were concerned.

If Hitler expected this wholesale terror and mayhem to return the National Socialists in overwhelming numbers to national legislature, he was mistaken. In the March 5th general election, 56 percent of those who dared to vote were brave enough to cast their votes against the Nazis. Forty-four percent of the ballots were cast for the National Socialist party, and 44 percent is not a majority.

By this time, however, the Reichstag and all that it represented were of no importance to the man who was taking power. Within a matter of weeks, whatever opposition there had been to Hitler collapsed. All legal parties, with the exception of the National Socialist party, were banned. Hitler was empowered to do what he willed with the constitution of the German Republic. He had thus become dictator of Germany.

When Ernst Roehm, leader of the two and a half million storm troopers, seemed to pose a threat to Hitler's absolute authority, the Fuehrer had him arrested and executed. At the Lichterfeld Cadet School, 150 top men of the S.A., suspected of disloyalty, were lined up against a wall and shot down by machine gun. There were hundreds of other storm troopers Hitler had rounded up and killed in mass execution. He would tolerate no possible deterrents to his supreme authority.

Numbers of leading German political figures, too, were brutally slain by order of Hitler or Goering. Ex-Chancellor Kurt von Schleicher and his wife were murdered. So was ex-Vice-Chancellor Gregor Strasser. Erich Klausener, Catholic Action leader, was murdered. Gustav Kahr, who had headed the anti-Republican government in Munich, was dumped into a swamp, his body punctured with ice-pick wounds. Father Bernhard Stemple, the priest who had helped Hitler with his *Mein Kampf,* was tossed into the woods after three bullets had been pumped into his heart and his neck broken.

"If anyone reproaches me," said Hitler, "all I can say [is] in this hour I was responsible for the fate of the German people. Everyone must know for all future time that if he raises his hand to strike the State, then certain death is his lot."

The State was Hitler. No one could make a mistake about that. One might speculate, then, on why Hitler did not have van der Lubbe, Dimitrov, Torgler, Popov, and Tanev executed at once. Certainly there was no one in all Germany to stop him.

It may have been international opinion that deterred him from doing so at the time. For the whole world had been shocked by the Reichstag fire and was concerned with who had caused it and why. More likely, however, Hitler saw the trial as a way of justifying his taking over control of Germany.

He was certain that the accusation against the Communists would hold up in court, especially in a court controlled by his own hirelings. In fact, he was so sure of this that he invited newspapermen, lawyers, ambassadors, and other dignitaries from all over the world to witness the trial. The trial and the conviction of the accused, Hitler calculated, would serve to show that he was a dedicated world leader in the fight against world communism. Indeed, it would also serve to demonstrate that he was the savior and rightful leader of the German people.

But Hitler's judgment in the matter turned out to be completely wrong. The trial was to prove a fiasco. Rather than condemn the Communists and bring glory to Hitler in the eyes of the world, it condemned the Nazis and certainly added dishonor to their already dishonorable leader.

The Trial

Judge Paul Vogt was the preliminary judge selected for the trial of the five men accused of setting the fire in the Reichstag. It was his job to collect all material pertinent to the crime, hear the testimony of the witnesses, and deliver a report on his findings to the prosecuting attorney. He was, in fact, handpicked by the Nazis for this task.

Vogt was almost a caricature of a proper Prussian official. He was arrogant and full of self-confidence. If he came to a decision, dynamite could not swerve him from it. He was a stickler for justice and had little acquaintance with the quality of mercy. And he knew his law.

But Judge Vogt, like everyone else in Germany in 1933, had to be concerned with the approval of the Nazi overlords. No one could detect direct Nazi pressure on the way he conducted his courtroom examination, but the indirect pressure was quite evident almost every step of the way.

Vogt did honor the several requests to investigate possible Nazi involvement in the Reichstag fire, but quickly discarded them after hearing the alibis presented by the several Nazis named. Yet no alibi offered by the Communists was allowed to acquit them of the charge made against them. In fact, Vogt accepted the Nazi version concerning the guilt of the Reichstag fire without reservation.

For five months, at the order of Judge Vogt, the accused men were brought in chains into the courthouse. The chains were heavy and painful, and it was illegal to force the prisoners to wear them. This was called to the attention of the judge on several occasions, but he did nothing about it. It was not until the actual trial had begun that the Communist prisoners had

A view of the judges at the Reichstag fire trial. Judge Vogt is at center.

their chains removed. But van der Lubbe wore his chains to the very end.

A large reward was offered to anyone who brought useful evidence to the court. The offer brought a stream of bogus "witnesses." Most of them turned out to be liars, thieves, and people simply eager to get their names and faces into the newspapers. Judge Vogt was not very discriminating in this area. He put everything he heard into his reports. By June of 1933, he delivered the fruit of his labors to the office of the prosecutor. There were thirty-two volumes which were going to prove, for the most part, useless to the Nazi cause.

The trial itself began on September 21, 1933, in the city of Leipzig. It would be moved to Berlin and then back again to Leipzig during its course. Dr. Wilhelm Bunger was the presiding magistrate. There were four associate judges, Dr. Coenders, Dr. Froelich, Dr. Lersch, and Dr. Rusch. There were, in addition to a number of interested foreign observers, eighty-two foreign correspondents for eighty-two newspapers and magazines from all parts of the world.

Dr. Bunger had a fair reputation in the legal field and he started the trial with dignity and fairness. But his was a hopeless task. Time after time witnesses were exposed as liars and frauds. Evidence was consistently contradictory. The judge began to fumble, stumble, and finally to bungle the whole proceedings. Like Judge Vogt, he was unquestionably and constantly under pressure to deliver for the Nazis. He simply could not do it, particularly with the eyes and ears of the world focused on his court.

It turned out to be Georgi Dimitrov who helped make the discomfort of the presiding judge complete. He became, in fact, the hero of the trial. Dimitrov was fighting for his life on a trumped-up charge. He had nothing to lose. Moreover, he had

The trial gets under way. This is a judge's view of the courtroom with van der Lubbe in the dock guarded by a policeman.

complete contempt for both his accusers and his judges, and he made no effort to conceal it.

Dimitrov, acting as his own defense counsel, was always polite and courteous, but his attacks on the Nazis and his comments on the judges and the manner in which they were conducting the trial were sharp, bitter, and ironic. On one occasion he would declare that the verdict of the trial was already fixed, and not by the court. On another occasion, he accused the Nazis themselves of setting the Reichstag fire. Once, drawing considerable laughter in the courthouse, he said rather quietly but bluntly to the presiding judge: "Please allow me to say you are extremely nervous today."

And the only way the judge could stop the rapier-like wit and devastating irony of Dimitrov was to have him forcibly removed from the court. Dr. Bunger did this with regularity. But each time Dimitrov was hustled out of the courtroom, the case against him and his three Communist companions was further damaged. And each time Dimitrov was returned to face his judges, he seemed more refreshed and his tongue even sharper.

Probably because their case was going badly, with the foreign newspapers printing all the details of the proceedings, Hermann Goering and Joseph Goebbels, the Propaganda Minister, decided to put in an appearance at the trial as witnesses. If the judges and the prosecuting attorney were no match for the clever Dimitrov, Goering and Goebbels figured that they would be able to put the Bulgarian Communist in "his place." They were wrong.

Goering entered the courtroom in his usual flamboyant manner, dressed in a flashy uniform, belt, and high boots. The moment he appeared, judges, attorneys, and audience jumped to their feet and stretched out their arms in the "Heil Hitler" salute. But Dimitrov had as much contempt for Goering as he had for everyone concerned with his trial. Dimitrov cross-examined Goering as if he were just another of the petty thieves who had served as witnesses in the proceedings. Goering began politely enough, although he sarcastically remarked on Dimitrov's reputation as an "exceptionally bright fellow." But slowly Goering's temper gave way as the Bulgarian cleverly exposed the minister as an unreliable witness.

"You are greatly afraid of my questions, are you not?" Dimitrov said to the flustered Goering.

"You will be afraid when I catch you!" exploded Hitler's right-hand man. "You wait till I get you out of the power of this court, you crook!"

And with that, Goering stalked out of the room.

The press did not fail to note that Goering had all but admitted the innocence of Dimitrov. Nor did it omit his threat against the Bulgarian's life once the trial was ended.

Goering had done his cause no good; and Goebbels, while he did not lose his temper and made no threats, did not fare much better.

Time and time again, Dimitrov clearly showed that brutality, violence, and murder were weapons of the National Socialist party; and Goebbels had no satisfactory rebuttal to these charges. All the Propaganda Minister could do was plead with the members of the foreign press to "cease publishing vile slanders about a decent, diligent and honorable people" — the Nazis.

The press was not impressed. On the contrary, the case against all the defendants, with the exception of van der Lubbe,

Above, Reichstag president Hermann Goering giving his deposition before the court. Below, Dr. Joseph Goebbels gives his testimony.

72

A view of the prisoners' box at the trial. Note that the accused were not allowed to sit together but were separated by police guards. Torgler and van der Lubbe are seated in the second row. Behind them, from left, are Popov, Tanev, and Dimitrov.

grew weaker and weaker. In time, it became obvious to the world that the Communists were not responsible for the Reichstag fire.

Indeed, van der Lubbe was an almost forgotten figure in the trial. He was brought to court in chains every day, and seemed to sit in a stupor throughout the proceedings. When he was questioned, it was always the same story. He had had no accomplices. He had worked alone. He, alone, had set fire to the Reichstag.

The trial lasted for just about two months. From the beginning, it had been obvious that the government had no case against any of the defendants except the unhappy van der Lubbe. Nevertheless, the verdict, when the judges delivered it, was something of a surprise.

Torgler, Dimitrov, Popov, and Tanev, the four Communists, were found not guilty and were acquitted. Marinus van der Lubbe was found guilty of high treason and sentenced to death.

The surprise was not in the harsh sentence meted out to van der Lubbe. The surprise was the courage of the judges who, despite the obvious Nazi pressure, gave freedom to the arch enemies and accusers of the National Socialist party. To all intents and purposes, the judges had accepted and put their stamp of approval on world opinion: the Reichstag fire had not been the signal for a Communist insurrection; on the contrary, it had probably been started by the Nazis themselves and used as a pretext to seize complete control of Germany.

Nazi leaders are sentenced during the final session of the War Crimes Trial at Nuremberg in 1946.

Postlude

Ernst Torgler, immediately after he had been acquitted, was arrested and thrown into a Nazi prison, where he died during World War II. The three Bulgarians managed to get back to their country. Later, Georgi Dimitrov became Prime Minister of Bulgaria. Marinus van der Lubbe was executed by decapitation on January 10, 1934.

On August 2nd of that year, the aged General Paul von Hindenburg died peacefully in his bed. Immediately Hitler proclaimed the merging of the presidency and the chancellorship into one office. The Fuehrer was now Head of State and Supreme Commander-in-Chief of the Reich's armed forces. Not a voice was raised in protest.

"In the next thousand years," Hitler declared in triumph, "there will be no other revolution in Germany."

That was in September 1934.

On April 30, 1945, with Germany defeated and the Allied armies moving quickly on Berlin, Hitler, according to reports, put a bullet into his head, and his gasoline-soaked body was burned beyond recognition. Paul Joseph Goebbels also died by his own hand in 1945 taking a dose of poison. At the Nuremburg Trials Hermann Goering was tried and found guilty of committing war crimes. He was condemned to be hanged but he beat the hangman by just two hours. He had swallowed a vial of poison which he had concealed on his person. He had cheated justice, perhaps; but he was dead.

Hitler's mania for power, for the law and order he envisioned, for a German military and industrial supremacy, and for a German conquest of the world had destroyed the German Republic after little more than a stormy and troubled decade. And he had also led the German people to a calamitous defeat, a crippling dismemberment, and a devastating humiliation.

Bibliography

Bullock, Alan. *A Study in Tyranny*. New York: Harper & Row, 1952.

Carr, W. *History of Germany*. New York: St. Martin's Press, 1969.

Heiden, Konrad. *Der Fuehrer*. Boston: Beacon Press, 1969.

Hitler, Adolf. *Mein Kampf*. New York: Reynal and Hitchcock, 1939.

Shirer, William. *Rise and Fall of the Third Reich*. New York: Simon and Schuster, 1960.

Simon, Walter. *Germany*. New York: Random House, 1966.

Speer, Albert. *Inside the Third Reich*. New York: Macmillan, 1970.

Index

About
the Author

Henry Gilfond, a free-lance writer, has taught in New York City junior high schools, edited literary and dance magazines, written for radio and television, and done reviews for the New York Times Book Review Section. He has written two plays, as well as a number of books and short stories. He lives in New York City with his wife, a costume designer for a daytime television show.